CIHM
Microfiche
Series
(Monographs)

ICMH
Collection de
microfiches
(monographies)

Canadian Institute for Historical Microreproductions / Institut canadien de microreproductions historiques

© 1996

Technical and Bibliographic Notes / Notes technique et bibliographiques

The Institute has attempted to obtain the best original copy available for filming. Features of this copy which may be bibliographically unique, which may alter any of the images in the reproduction, or which may significantly change the usual method of filming are checked below.

L'Institut a microfilmé le meilleur exemplaire qu'il lui a été possible de se procurer. Les détails de cet exemplaire qui sont peut-être uniques du point de vue bibliographique, qui peuvent modifier une image reproduite, ou qui peuvent exiger une modifications dans la méthode normale de filmage sont indiqués ci-dessous.

☐ Coloured covers /
Couverture de couleur

☐ Covers damaged /
Couverture endommagée

☐ Covers restored and/or laminated /
Couverture restaurée et/ou pelliculée

☐ Cover title missing / Le titre de couverture manque

☐ Coloured maps / Cartes géographiques en couleur

☐ Coloured ink (i.e. other than blue or black) /
Encre de couleur (i.e. autre que bleue ou noire)

☐ Coloured plates and/or illustrations /
Planches et/ou illustrations en couleur

☐ Bound with other material /
Relié avec d'autres documents

☐ Only edition available /
Seule édition disponible

☐ Tight binding may cause shadows or distortion along interior margin / La reliure serrée peut causer de l'ombre ou de la distorsion le long de la marge intérieure.

☐ Blank leaves added during restorations may appear within the text. Whenever possible, these have been omitted from filming / Il se peut que certaines pages blanches ajoutées lors d'une restauration apparaissent dans le texte, mais, lorsque cela était possible, ces pages n'ont pas été filmées.

☐ Additional comments /
Commentaires supplémentaires:

☐ Coloured pages / Pages de couleur

☐ Pages damaged / Pages endommagées

☐ Pages restored and/or laminated /
Pages restaurées et/ou pelliculées

☑ Pages discoloured, stained or foxed /
Pages décolorées, tachetées ou piquées

☐ Pages detached / Pages détachées

☑ Showthrough / Transparence

☐ Quality of print varies /
Qualité inégale de l'impression

☐ Includes supplementary material /
Comprend du matériel supplémentaire

☐ Pages wholly or partially obscured by errata slips, tissues, etc., have been refilmed to ensure the best possible image / Les pages totalement ou partiellement obscurcies par un feuillet d'errata, une pelure, etc., ont été filmées à nouveau de façon à obtenir la meilleure image possible.

☐ Opposing pages with varying colouration or discolourations are filmed twice to ensure the best possible image / Les pages s'opposant ayant des colorations variables ou des décolorations sont filmées deux fois afin d'obtenir la meilleure image possible.

This item is filmed at the reduction ratio checked below/
Ce document est filmé au taux de réduction indiqué ci-dessous.

10X		14X		18X		22X		26X		30X	
					✓						
	12X		16X		20X		24X		28X		32X

1	2	3

1
2
3

1	2	3
4	5	6

MICROCOPY RESOLUTION TEST CHART

(ANSI and ISO TEST CHART No. 2)

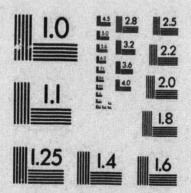

APPLIED IMAGE Inc

1653 East Main Street
Rochester, New York   14609   USA
(716) 482 – 0300 – Phone
(716) 288 – 5989 – Fax

The Coming of the Comforter

A SERMON

BY

REV. D. MACLEAN

225 Sidney Street
CHARLOTTETOWN, P. E. I.

1912

"And when the day of Pentecost was fully come, they were all with one accord in one place.

And suddenly there came a sound from heaven as of a rushing mighty wind, and it filled all the house where they were sitting.

And there appeared unto them cloven tongues like as of fire, and it sat upon each of them.

And they were all filled with the Holy Ghost, and began to speak with other tongues, as the Spirit gave them utterance."—Acts 2 : 1-4.

The Coming of the Comforter

"And when the day of Pentecost was fully come, they were all with one accord in one place.

And suddenly there came a sound from heaven as of a rushing mighty wind, and it filled all the house where they were sitting.

And there appeared unto them cloven tongues like as of fire, and it sat upon each of them.

And they were all filled with the Holy Ghost, and began to speak with other tongues, as the Spirit gave them utterance."—Acts 2 : 1-4.

Christ and His disciples had now been together about three years. They accompanied Him from place to place, heard Him preach and saw His miracles. He had instructed, counselled and comforted them ; and with all their waywardness they loved Him, Iscariot excepted. They thought that He was going to stay here always. But when He told them that He was going away to leave them in the world, they became very sad and sorrowful. Then He promised to send them another Comforter that would abide with them forever. The Comforter promised is the Holy Ghost, proceeding from the Father and the Son. This glorious truth is recorded in John 14, 15 and 16.

We read also that when the disciples were assembled with Christ for the last time, ere His ascension to Glory, He said unto them : "For John truly baptized with water ; but ye shall be baptized with the Holy Ghost not many days hence."— Acts 1 : 5 But ye shall receive power, after the Holy Ghost is come upon you ; and ye shall be witnesses unto me both in Jerusalem and in all Judea, and in Samaria, and unto the uttermost part of the earth.—Acts I : 8. He commanded them to tarry in Jerusalem till this blessed promise should be fulfilled unto them They obeyed His command, and they were not disappointed. The blessed day arrived when the Comforter, the Holy Spirit, came upon them to be in them and abide with them forever. The great need of the Church to-day is a baptism of the Holy Spirit. The promise of the out-pouring of the Spirit holds good in all gospel ages, and consequently to us of the present day ; and, if the promise is not fulfilled to us, the fault must be ours. But are we praying and looking for out-pourings of the Spirit as the disciples were on the day of Pentecost? I think it is safe to say that we are not, unless in very few cases ; hence the coldness and spiritual death that is in the Church. That there have been, and still are, times of refreshing in some places, we readily admit ; but, on the whole, there is room for great improvement in this respect. While learning and all other accomplishments are highly valued in the Church, the work of the Spirit is very often neglected, and sometimes ignored. If the Church is ever going to accomplish all that her great head has entrusted to her, she must give His proper place and honor to the Holy Spirit in the work of saving souls, which is her great work. This is a subject of vast importance, and we intend to say a little on it, and may the Holy Spirit enlighten and instruct us, and our words and thoughts be His, and God's the glory. Let us then realize the words of Christ, who said, "Without me ye can do nothing."

We will consider this glorious subject under the following heads :

    I.—Waiting for Christ's Promise.
    II.—Christ's Promise Fulfilled.
    III.—The Work of the Holy Spirit.

I.—Waiting for Christ's Promise

When Christ told His disciples that He was going away to the Father, they felt very sorry. Though they sometimes disobeyed His commands, owing to weaknesses and imperfections, yet they loved Him. Their opinion, like that of all Jews, was that he would always stay with them in this world, and build up a great kingdom in it, greater and grander than any kingdom or Empire that ever existed before, and that they themselves would be His first ministers. But when they heard that He was going away soon, and to leave them in the world, their hearts were filled with sorrow. They were much disappointed and cast down. Then He promised to send them another Comforter, the Spirit of truth, who should abide with them forever. He showed them that it was necessary for them that He should go to the Father ; that, unless He would go, the Comforter, the Holy Spirit, would not come to them, and that they ought rather to rejoice because He was going, that it would be a great benefit to them and not a loss, as they were thinking. —(Jno. 14 : 16, 26, 27 ; 15 : 26 ; 16 : 7.)

Shortly after this Christ was crucified, and rose again on the third day, and continued forty days on earth after His resurrection. But the day of His ascension to glory came. He commanded them at His last interview, to tarry at Jerusalem, and there wait the fulfilment of His Promise ; that the Comforter He had promised would come in a few days, and that they would be baptized with the Holy Ghost. They obeyed His command. They went to Jerusalem, and chose an upper room, and there awaited the fulfilment of the Saviour's promise, which promise He received from the Father, as a reward for His sufferings and death, and for the atonement He made, by which He satisfied Divine justice and purchased the gift of the Spirit, and salvation for lost and ruined sinners.

We will now consider how the disciples were engaged when waiting the fulfilment of Christ's promise. Their number was now increased to about one hundred and twenty. Probably Mary, the mother of our Lord, and the other holy women, are included in this number. Women were called disciples. Tabitha is called a disciple, Acts 9 : 36. The word disciple signifies a learner or follower.

As to how many were present on the day of Pentecost, we are not sure. Probably the disciples called together many of their kinsmen and near friends, as Cornelius did. The disciples were, no doubt, much happier because Judas Iscariot was not there, having gone to his own place—hell. Every society, church and neighborhood is better off when the wicked depart. Then there will be peace and quiet among them. The wicked cannot cease from troubling in this world. It is their nature and their delight.

They were with one accord in one place. Twelve apostles were there again, Matthias having been added to their number, and other men and women, with Mary, the mother of Jesus, and His brethren. This is the last time her name is mentioned in the sacred record. Certainly no pre-eminence is given her over others. The other women are mentioned first. Christ's relations according to the flesh, His mother and brethren, are mentioned last. God's children do not bear lordship over each other. They were looking eagerly for the coming of the Comforter, the Holy Spirit, according to Christ's promise. These all continued with one accord in prayer and supplication. They were intensely in earnest. Supplication means an earnest entreaty. They were praying and imploring God in their prayer. Now they were like lambs among wolves, their beloved head and teacher had departed. All were praying. The one needed the

Comforter as much as the other, the women as well as the men. Believers are all one in Christ Jesus. The Comforter was coming to the women as well as to the men. Women have souls to be saved as well as men, and they will glorify God in Heaven as much as men. They have as much place in the redemptive work of Christ and in the eternal love of God. They were all of one accord; this was as it should be. In this the beauty of the Lord God was upon them. There was no discord or bickering among them. The quarrels, discords and bickerings, that alas! too often obtain in the church are no doubt the cause of grieving away the Holy Spirit and preventing much good. The Holy Spirit is a spirit of love, peace, unity, and holiness; and He comes to impart these glorious blessings.

One absorbing thought pervaded that loving assembly. It was the coming of the Comforter. For His coming they looked, for His coming they prayed, for His coming they sighed and wept. They had full confidence in Him that promised and so continued day after day waiting the fulfilment of His promise. They were not weary of their meeting either. Oh! what a glorious thought it was, the coming of the third person of the glorious Trinity. It was the same in importance as the coming of Christ into the world; not an event of less importance, but of equal importance and blessedness. He is possessed of divine powers. He is going to dwell in the souls of men, enlighten and sanctify them. He is going to make Christ's work effectual to salvation, by applying to men the Redemption purchased by Him. Then He was coming to teach and to comfort; to make believers joyful and happy. If the Spirit is going to come to us in such power and with such fulness of blessings, we ought to wait for His coming into our hearts as they did. He is our Comforter as well as theirs. Be filled with the spirit.—Eph. 5; 18. The Comforter was coming to endue them with power from on high, to prepare them to face every danger fearlessly, and overcome the world triumphantly.

II.—Christ's Promise Fulfilled

The faithful assembly of praying men and women waited patiently for ten days. They were bound to get the promised blessing, and fully believed that they would get it. It is probable enough that flesh and blood told them, more than once, that they had waited long enough, that it was time to give up. Nevertheless they persevered. The promised gift was a Divine and Heavenly one.

On the tenth day Christ's promise was fulfilled to them. It was the day of Pentecost, the first day of the week, which is the Christian Sabbath or the Lord's Day.

Pentecost was one of the three great Jewish festivals and lasted but one day. Pentecost is a Greek word and means fifty (days). It occurs only in the New Testament. In the Old Testament it is called the Feast of Weeks and the Feast of Harvest. The Jews hold that the Feast of Pentecost was instituted to commemorate the giving of the law on Mount Sinai, and some commentators have adopted their view. But this cannot be proved, and the fact that no mention was made of it when the feast was instituted militates greatly against it. (See Lev. 23 Ch.) This great feast was celebrated at the close of the wheat harvest, as a public thanksgiving to God for the bounties of His Providence. The Feast of Weeks occurred at the end of seven weeks from the second day of the Passover, and hence fifty days after the Passover Sabbath.—(Lev. 23 : 15, 16.) These weeks were the harvest time in Palestine, corresponding to

, to
and

uen
to
hat
esh
had
up.
gift

ul-
rst
or

ish
ek
he
ed
he
to
ai,
w.
n-
ni-
nis
at
he
ks
nd
ne
ks
to

our May with some days of April and June. It began
with the offering of the first sheaf of the barley harvest
in the Passover, and ended with the offering of the
first two loaves of the wheat harvest. The flour was
to be that of the land, and the loaves leavened. The
offering of these loaves was the distinguishing rite of
Pentecost. They were waved by the Priest before the
Lord; and was an occasion of great rejoicing. Free
will offerings were made to the Lord, according as
the Lord had blessed them. It was the second of the
three great Jewish festivals. All the family, the
stranger, the orphan and widow, and the levites feast-
ed and rejoiced together. Everything was done on a
liberal scale. How significant these loaves were of
Christ the bread of life, waved in the preaching of the
Gospel. They were the first-fruits of the wheat harvest.
Christ is the grain of wheat that fell into the ground,
died, and bore much fruit. He died but arose.
Pentecost also occurred on the fiftieth day after Christ's
resurrection. Devout Jews from every country in the
world came home to attend this great feast, and
Proselytes from all gentile nations—hence there was
a great concourse of people in Jerusalem, speaking
many languages.

While the little flock were still engaged in prayer
and supplication, suddenly there came a sound from
Heaven as of a rushing mighty wind, which filled the
house where they were sitting. This was the manner
of the Comforter's coming. He came in a wonderful
and, no doubt, in an unexpected way. The sound
came from Heaven and filled the house. The mighty
wind showed power, yea, an unseen power. The
Holy Spirit is compared to three of the four elements
of nature, namely, wind, fire, and water; but not to
the earth. In His powerful operation here He is
compared to the wind. The wind moves and blows,
and in this shows energy and power. Then the wind is
absolute in its operations and movements, and so is

the Holy Spirit. He worketh where and how He wills. Sound awakens those asleep. The Spirit has an awakening power. This rushing sound as of a mighty wind prepared them to receive the Spirit; it could not but put them into a serious, reverential frame of mind. They were mightily stirred up as they said to themselves now He is coming. Here He is! we shall see Him. They saw Him in a symbol, not probably as they expected. There is a preparatory work ere men receive the Holy Spirit. Conviction goes before conversion. The law must be preached to people if they are going to be awakened. Though it was not in the mighty rushing wind that the Lord came to Elijah, yet it prepared him to hear the still small voice. The Lord commanded Ezekiel to prophesy unto the wind and say, "Thus saith the Lord God; Come from the four winds, O breath."—Ezek. 37:9. The Spirit, in some of His operations, is compared to the wind, to a mighty rushing wind. Great is the power of the Holy Spirit, glorious is His work! It is the Spirit that awakens sinners to a sense of their lost and ruined condition, and imparts spiritual life to their dead souls. First came the sound from Heaven. This was the first intimation of the Comforter's glorious coming.

Then a wonderful sight, there appeared unto them cloven tongues like as of fire, which sat upon each of them. This was the visible manifestation of the coming of the Comforter. The Holy Spirit is mentioned first in Gen. 1:2.—"And the Spirit of God moved upon the face of the waters." The three persons of the Trinity were engaged in the creation of all things. The Father created all things by the Son, and the Son created all things by the agency and power of the Spirit. The Holy Spirit by His divine power affected or touched matter and gave shape, form, and beauty to it; gave all their beauty to the earth and Heavens; garnished the Heavens with sun, moon and stars; gave them their shining glory and moving power. But all the work of creation was done co-ordinately by the three persons of the Trinity, and not seperate ; they are one in all things ; the one is not alone or without the other in any part of the glorious work of creation. The persons of the Godhead are not subordinate or inferior to each other in their glorious work. Though the Son subordinated himself by taking our nature upon Him and becoming man, yet with regard to His Divine nature He was unchangeable and eternal and co-equal to the Father.

When Satan captured the whole world through the fall of man, the Holy Spirit had not much place in it. Satan the evil spirit came to dwell in the world, and move to and fro in it. The Holy Spirit was still striving with men, but was not seen in the world any more till He descended on Christ at His Baptism.

The Son proceeded from the Father only, but the Holy Spirit, the Comforter, proceeded, and proceeds, from the Father and the Son. He is spoken of in Scripture as the Spirit of the Father, and the Spirit of Christ. He is also called the Spirit of Truth, the Holy Spirit, the Holy Ghost and the Comforter. Both the Father and the Son are revealed where the Holy Spirit is, and there they put forth their power.

The Holy Spirit descended upon Christ in bodily shape at His Baptism. And Jesus, when He was baptized, went up straightway out of the water, and, lo, the Heavens were opened unto Him, and He saw the Spirit descending like a dove and lighting upon Him. Christ as the Son of God needed not the Spirit, but he had become man, and as Mediator He needed the Holy Spirit with Him in His work. It was by the Holy Spirit that He was going to preach, cast out devils, and impart spiritual life unto men. He received gifts for men. Then we have in Jno. 1 ; 33.—And

I knew Him not; but He that sent me to baptize with water, the same said unto me, upon whom thou shalt see the Spirit descending, and remaining on Him, the same is He which baptizeth with the Holy Ghost. Christ then baptizes with Holy Ghost. The Holy Ghost was seen three times figuratively. Some one might contend that He was not seen by mortal eye at the creation. But that He moved upon the face of the waters, is recorded in the word of God, and we must believe it, and what we believe, we see by faith. Faith sees afar. The Spirit of God moved upon the face of the waters.—Gen. 1: 2. The word moved is also translated hovered or brooded; that is, moved as a bird over the vast expanse of water. The only bird that is symbolic of the Holy Spirit is the dove; and at the new creation the Spirit came down on Christ's head in bodily shape as a dove. He it is that creates anew. We are created anew by the power of the Holy Spirit. The church of Christ is a new creation. If anyone is in Christ Jesus, he is a new creature. Behold I make all things new. Why like the dove? Because the dove was the only clean bird used in sacrifices, and is innocent and beautiful. He is a fitting emblem of the Holy Spirit, as the lamb is of Christ.

We come now to the coming of the Comforter on the day of Pentecost. When the sound from Heaven had filled the house, there appeared unto them cloven tongues like as of fire, and it sat upon each of them. This was the visible sign that accompanied the Baptism of the Holy Ghost. It was a beautiful symbol of the burning energy and perfect purity of the Holy Spirit descending upon the Church, and about to pour himself through every tongue and nation on earth. The appearance of the living jets or flames of fire, cloven and of the shape of human tongues, was most significant and beautiful.

The Holy Spirit consumes sin as fire consumes dross, and imparts zeal, purity and holiness to precious souls, creating in them an inexpressible glory exceeding the sun in its noon day splendor. They were filled with the Holy Ghost. The Comforter came in all His blessed Heavenly powers. The promise of the Father was fulfilled:

"I will pour out my spirit upon Him that is thirsty, and floods upon the dry ground; I will pour out my spirit on thy seed, and my blessing upon thine offspring.—Is. 44 : 3 ;

And I will pour upon the house of David, and upon the inhabitants of Jerusalem, the spirit of grace and supplication.—Zech. 12 : 10.

And it shall come to pass afterward that I will pour out my spirit upon all flesh ; and your sons and your daughters shall prophesy, your old men shall dream dreams, your young men shall see visions.

And also upon the servants and upon the handmaids in those days will I pour out my spirit."—Joel 2 : 28, 29 ;

And I will give them one heart, and I will put a new spirit within you ; and I will take the stoney heart out of your flesh, and I will give them an heart of flesh.—Ezek. 11 : 19 ;

And I will put my spirit within you and cause you to walk in my statutes, and ye shall keep my judgments, and do them.—Ezek. 36 : 27.

He that believeth in me as the scripture hath said, out of his belly shall flow rivers of living water. But this he spake of the spirit which they that believe on him should receive."—Jno. 7 : 38, 39.

The passages relative to the sending, giving and coming of the Comforter in Jno. 14 : 26 ; 15 : 26 ; 16, 7, 13, I have already quoted, and the reader can see them for himself.

The persons of the blessed and glorious Trinity are not seperate in the work of redemption, though each performing a distinct part. The Father was with the Son, as Christ said: "I am not alone, because the Father is with me."—Jno. 16:32. The only exception to this was the time when Christ was suffering in the room of sinners, when the Father hid His face from Him. But this was necessary, because the work was given to Christ to perform, that the glory of the work might be His own. The awful cloud of our sins enveloped Christ for a little while, and the Father's wrath fell on Him for the sins of others. But Christ made an end of the sins of believers and the cloud of sin vanished forever. Then came to Him the sunshine of the Father's favor for all eternity. And yet in the hour of His sufferings there was a sense in which the Father was with Him. The Father was interested in His Son personally and in the work He was accomplishing. The Father is glorified in the work of the Son, and the Son in the work of the Spirit. All the three persons are rejoicing in each other's work. No part of creation or redemption is subordinate, but of equal importance.

The Comforter then appeared as flames of light, or burning fire, signifying the nature of the work he was to do, and His power to do it. Fire has a purifying power. Gold is refined in the fire. The Holy Spirit purifies us; consumes our dross. Of our sins He makes an end by sanctifying us wholly. As fire imparts heat, the Spirit imparts zeal to believers, making them zealous of good works and the cause of Christ. As the fire gives light, so the Spirit gives spiritual light. Great is the darkness of sin, and sin has made mankind ignorant, stubborn and wicked. The Holy Spirit imparts knowledge of God and of ourselves. The Spirit puts all Divine graces into our souls, and makes us anew. Thus believers are made Christ-like. Where the Spirit of Christ is not, there is but spiritual death, corruption and sin; but where the Holy Spirit is, there is joy, peace, love, spiritual life, purity and holiness.

Christ had before the day of Pentecost breathed on His disciples and said unto them, receive ye the Holy Ghost.—Jno. 20 : 22. This was but an earnest of what they would soon receive. To him that hath, more will be given. This token He gave them ere His ascension to glory. This cheered and comforted them, and gave them an earnest desire for the fulness of the Spirit.

III.—The Work of the Holy Spirit

The faithful little flock who were anxiously waiting were filled with the Holy Ghost. The Comforter came to them in all His blessed powers, and the first result was that they spoke with tongues. The theme of those filled with the Holy Ghost was the wonderful works of God. All who were waiting for the fulfilment of Christ's promise were filled with the Spirit, probably one hundred and twenty, and they began to speak of the wonderful works of God. The wonderful works of God here mentioned were, no doubt the Redemption by Christ; the great salvation He had accomplished for men, the prescious blood; the forgiveness of sin, and all the glorious blessings of the Gospel. They praised and magnified God for those great things, and exhorted and instructed others earnestly, weeping tears of joy, with exclamations of praises to God. This is the outcome of the spirit in the hearts of men. When Peter preached in Cornelius' house, those on whom the Holy Spirit fell spoke with tongues and magnified God. When Elizabeth was filled with the Holy Ghost she spoke out with a loud voice; and Mary said, my soul doth magnify the Lord, and my spirit hath rejoiced in God my Saviour.—Luke 1: 41, 46, 47. The Christian professors who has not shed tears of joy and gladness, and who has not praised and magnified the Lord, nor spoken of redemption to others, is to be pitied. He is more like an icicle than a Christian.

The company assembled in the upper room were not of the learned class I think it is safe to say that none of them were possessed of classical education. They were but common men and women, and of the poorer class at that. But the Lord has chosen the poor of this world rich in faith. They were all speaking with tongues, and declaring the wonderful works of God.

And soon the news spread abroad, and a multitude came to see and hear what was going on in the city. Curiosity has nimble feet. The vastness of the crowd that gathered is proved from the fact that three thousand of them were converted that day. Three thousand is quite a large congregation, and it is but a reasonable inference that there were a great many present who were not converted then. There were a great many people from many countries in Jerusalem at that season of the year, and some of them devout men and women from many different nations. There were soon gathered around the faithful flock a great concourse of people, a mixed multitude from all nations. These were very much astonished when they heard those poor Gallileans speaking in every language that was represented there, and many languages were spoken by them. There were present Parthians, Medes, and Elamites, and dwellers in Mesopotamia, and Judea, Cappadocia, Pontus and Asia, Phrygia, Pamphylia, Egypt, Lybia, Cyrene and Rome, Jews and Prosetyles, Cretes and Arabians. They were from Asia, Europe and Africa. But they heard these Gallileans speak in their own mother tongue, and they were very much astonished, and

an pro-
adness,
rd, nor
d. He

n were
ly that
cation,
of the
en the
speak-
works

multi-
in the
of the
three
Three
but a
many
ere a
salem
evout
There
great
all
they
very
many
esent
s in
and
and
ians,
they
ther
and

when they went away spread the Gospel in many countries, by declaring the wonderful things they had seen and heard. They never heard the like before; there never was the like in the world before. The wickedness and folly of men caused the confusion of tongues at the building of the tower of Babel. The Holy Spirit restored the language of men to what it ought to be, and to what it will, no doubt, be in Heaven, where we will all know and understand each other. When sin and all its effects will be removed, we shall all be of one language, as well as of one heart and one spirit. They were all wondering what all this meant; but some put a bad construction upon it, saying that they were but drunken men and women. The ignorant and wicked will always interpret things in a bad way. But Peter reasoned them out of the mistake by pointing out that it was but the third hour of the day, corresponding to our nine o'clock in the morning, ours being the Roman method of computation. The Jews reckoned the hours of the day from sunrise to sunset. He showed them that it was out of the question for people to be drunken so early; but that it was the fulfillment of Prophecy. The first fruits of the Comforter was the power of speaking with tongues, and praising and glorifying God, to the astonishment of the world.

This was a glorious day, the beginning of the ministry of the Spirit, by which men are equipped to go forth and preach the everlasting Gospel to a perishing world. God's servants were and are fully prepared for the work of the ministry, and the service of God in all departments of the glorious work of saving souls and glorifying God.

We have already referred to the Spirit's work in the creation of the world. We will here refer briefly to His work in the creation of men and animals, and more at large to His part of the redemptive work. He

fashioned the bodies of men and animals, and
body of our Lord Jesus Christ, whose concept
was by the power of the Holy Ghost.

We will now consider His work in the redempt
of mankind: When He (the Comforter) is come,
will reprove the world of sin and of righteousness,
judgment.—Jno. 16: 8. In the Revised Version
word, reprove, is translated convict. The Gr
word may be translated reprove, convict, rebuke,
The word convince is that which expresses more f
the work of the Spirit upon a sinful world.

Conviction is a work of the Holy Spirit. Man
counsel, rebuke, explain, argue, lecture, and prea
but it is the Spirit only that can convince. The H
Spirit alone can open the heart. The Spirit convir
by the word and conscience. The servants of C
speak the word. The ministry is set apart for th
but it may be done by any one of the Godly as w
They can exhort and rebuke. The Comforter t
convinces first, and then comforts; first wounds,
then applies the healing balm. He will silence
adversaries of the Lord Jesus, and show them the f
and wickedness of opposing Him and His cause,
showing them the truth and excellency of that wh
they oppose. Many have been, and are still, conv
ed of their sins and turn to the Lord, and get sa
tion; others are convinced against their will, opp
the spirit, give room to the devil, continue in sin,
perish. Man can harden his own heart by resis
the Holy Ghost, as the unbelieving Jews did.
works that Christ did in the world,—His glor
miracles—proved that He was the Son of God.
the Scribes and Pharisees, who were Jews, were
mad at Christ and His convincing miracles that t
attributed them to Beelzebub, the prince of
devils. It is possible for men to become awl
wicked in this present world. In their eagernes

als, and the
conception

redemption
is come, He
ousness, and
Version the
The Greek
rebuke, etc.
more fully

, Man can
d preach ;
The Holy
convinces
ts of God
t for that ;
y as well.
rter then
unds, and
lence the
n the folly
cause, by
hat which
, convinc-
get salva-
l, oppose
sin, and
resisting
id. The
glorious
od. But
were so
hat they
of the
awfully
rness to

be avenged on Christ, they committed the unpardonable sin and destroyed themselves for time and eternity. The preaching of the Gospel by the disciples, and the miracles they worked, were convincing on the world ; the preaching of the Gospel to-day, and its influences are convincing sinners that it is of God, and from Heaven ; the holy lives of the Godly are of a convincing nature, and all is by the Spirit, who has imparted holiness and grace to believers. The Holy Spirit shall convince the world of sin, the wickedness of sin, the folly of sin, and of the just punishment of sin, and of the impure fountain of sin, our corrupt human nature, and of the defiling nature of sin, and of the wrath of God against sin, and of the justice of that wrath. We mean by *world* here, the world of the ungodly, which is in a perishing state.

1. "Of sin because they believe not on me."— Jno. 16: 9. Unbelief is the great fountain of all sin; that which kept so many of Israel out of the land of promise, and is keeping the world to-day from entering into the rest of Faith here, and the eternal rest of Heaven hereafter. The Comforter strikes at the root of the great evil in the world, in order to remove it, break it down, that sinners may see what sin is, and know and feel that they are sinners, and look to Christ, believe in Him, and get salvation. Oh ! glorious work of the divine and glorious Comforter. How blessed that He has come. Glory be to the Father and to the Son for His coming !

2. He shall convince the world of righteousness, because, says Christ, I go to my Father, and ye see me no more. That God the Father received Him back to glory was a proof that He was the Son of God. This merely is a proof that He was righteous, and no imposter, as men tried to prove. They said that He deceived the people, that He was a Samaritan and had a devil. Sufficient witnesses saw Him ascending to

glory. The coming of the Comforter which He promised was a proof that He was truly all that He claimed to be. That Christ is seen no more in the likeness of sinful flesh, or as a man of sorrows and trials, proves His righteousness. The Holy Spirit convinces men that they are sinful and need righteousness, and teaches them where righteousness is to be found, that they may look to Jesus, receive His righteousness, and become Holy men of God.

3. "He (the Comforter) will convince the world of judgment, because the Prince of this world is judged." Satan is the Prince of this world. The Comforter discovers to men that Satan is a great deceiver and destroyer of men's souls and bodies. He has convinced many of this truth, and has led many to look to Christ for righteousness. Christ by the work of the Comforter is destroying the kingdom of Satan in the world by casting him out of the souls and bodies of men. The Holy Spirit by regenerating and sanctifying men breaks down Satan's kingdom. Satan was seen as lightening fell from Heaven. He caused the fall of mankind by his lies and wickedness, but Christ by His finished work, His holy spirit and truth, has given Satan a great fall in this world, by casting him out of his possessions and breaking up his kingdom. He is judged now in this world, and will finally be judged in the last great day. The light of God's word, the work of the Spirit, and the success of the kingdom of God in the world judges Satan and his work. Satan is being cast out; glory to God in the highest!

4. The Comforter is also called the Spirit of Truth. He it is that guides us into all truth; He causes us to understand the truth, and guides us in the way to the truth. We are sanctified by the Holy Spirit. The Comforter resides in the souls of men and there puts forth His glorious powers in the sanctification and en-

lightenment of men. Sanctify means to make holy, and it is the work of the Holy Spirit by removing sin, and making straight what Satan made crooked, and giving form to that which Satan deformed; that is, making us anew in the image of Christ. He imparts unto us light to see ourselves as sinners, and what Satan by sin made us, shows us the excellencies of Christ and creates in us desires to be like Him. This is the desire of every Godly one; hence the Godly mourn over their deformity, and oh! to be Christ like is their prayer and cry.

5. Reviving and refreshing are the work of the Comforter. Believers sometimes grow cold in spiritual things, but the Holy Spirit revives and quickens and refreshes them. A tear comes again unto our eyes, and spiritual emotions into our hearts. The Holy Spirit has caused it. We are revived again; we get happy once more, and feel again a little of the joys of our new birth. Thus we are helped in this sinful world; it is comforting that we are travelling to the land where joy and happiness are full. These revivings and refreshings are to us an earnest of the bliss of Heaven.

The spirit, as the word Comforter signifies, comforts. In our sorrow and dependency, we need comfort, and none can comfort like the Holy Spirit. When we have bereavements and disappointments, the Spirit comforts us. When we are dejected and cast down, the Holy Spirit comes with His blessed consolations. He can use the promises to comfort us. We cannot sink into despair when the Spirit is comforting us. In sickness and pain, when He fills our heart, we are strengthened and helped. In death the Holy Spirit brings the best comfort. His presence can make the Godly rejoice in their last moments. They may truly say, though I walk through the valley of the shadow of death, I will fear no evil.

The fruits of the Spirit are clearly stated in Gal. 5 : 22. "But the fruit of the Spirit is love, joy, peace, long-suffering, gentleness, goodness, faith, meekness, temperance." What beautiful fruits! How blessed are those bearing them. They truly live to the praise of God, and are beautiful in His sight. He sees no iniquity in Jacob nor perverseness in His spiritual Israel. The Comforter glorifies Christ. He receives of His. God the Father glorified His Son in Heaven, and God the Spirit on earth. All the gifts and graces of the Spirit; all that the Spirit bestows upon the Church came through Christ. The Father gave them to Christ as the reward of His obedience and sufferings, and Christ entrusts them to the Spirit to bestow upon His people. But Christ purchased them all.

When a soul is saved and renewed by the Holy Spirit, God is glorified. Another bright one, in the image of Christ, begins to moves Heavenward. The kingdom of God is increased. Then there is rejoicing in Heaven over sinners converted and returning. The Spirit makes Christ's work effectual by applying to us the redemption purchased by the Divine Saviour. The Three Persons of the Trinity rejoice in each other ; and in the salvation of lost sinners. It is possible to resist the Holy Ghost, Christ said to the Jews, ye do always resist the Holy Ghost. When the Holy Ghost is grieved away He will then return no more. He may indeed stay long and endure much before He finally leaves.

We cannot adequately express the glorious work of the Holy Spirit on the day of Pentecost. Oh! most glorious day. Before the close of that eventful day about three thousand converts were added to church. I think we may truly say that so many was never converted in one day before. They were all preaching, Peter leading and giving the principal discourse ; but the rest were praying and praising God. Their hearts were filled with the Holy Ghost, and their words were directed by Him. They were all praising and blessing God and exhorting others. They were all at work preaching, praising, and baptizing. There was plenty to do, and they were able and willing to do it.

The Comforter, the Holy Ghost is possessed of all divine attributes. He is *omnipotent*, that is, possessed of infinite power. The literal meaning of this word is all power. He is *omnipresent*; that is, present everywhere. He is omniscient, that is, He has all knowledge. These attributes are divine powers and belong not to a created being. All divine powers belong equally to each person of the Holy Trinity. The Holy Spirit is not simply an influence, as some have supposed, but a person. He wills and works where and how He wills. He takes of the things of Christ and presents them. A person *only* can exercise a will. That which any person of the Trinity wills and proposes, is the will and purpose of all Three Persons. They are in perfect harmony in all things, and can never differ in anything. They are perfectly one in all things. What the Spirit wills, the Father and the Son wills. Their wills move and act together, being one.

The Comforter is called the Spirit of Truth, which proceedeth from the Father.—Jno. 15 : 26. The rays of the sun, which radiate from it, do not separate from the sun, but are ever one with it; so the Comforter's proceeding to us with all His blessed light and influence does not cause any change with reference to His unity and presence with the Father and the Son. He acts, wills, and testifies, which are functions of a person.—(I Jno. 5 : 8.) He inspired the Apostles to speak and write, and work miracles. The work of the Spirit testified of Christ, and still testifies. The work of the Spirit proves Him divine, and that He who sent Him is none other than the Son of God.

We will now say a little with regard to the desirableness of getting spiritual blessings ; such as came on the day of Pentecost. If we are ever to get such glorious blessings we must seek them earnestly. We do not expect to see the Spirit descending like tongues of fire. Nevertheless He maketh His ministers a flame of fire ; nor do we expect to speak with other tongues ; but we shall expect to speak the language of Canaan. If we speak that, it is better than if we spoke a thousand other tongues. How blessed it is to be God's spiritual children, to speak in the Spirit is the best tongue. None can do this but those in whom the Holy Spirit dwells.

Some years ago a great revival in Eastern Ontario had its beginning in the prayers of a few little school girls. They felt their need of prayer and at recess went to a bush nearby to pray together. They found it interesting, told their companions, and they joined them, and it spread to the whole school, and from the school to the church. And by and by the whole country side was ablaze with a glorious revival. It was a blessed out-pouring of the Spirit. A glorious time of refreshing which came in answer to prayer. The great revival in Wales, a few years ago was, we have been informed, in answer to the prayers of poor humble Godly men and women. They were praying for a revival, and in God's good time and way it came. It was a Pentecostal blessing. God loves to answer the prayers of His people, young and old.

The Fulton Street Prayer Meeting in New York has been greatly blessed, and has been a great blessing to many. Business men and others in trouble and anxiety resorted to it, to pray or ask others to pray for them. There they poured out their hearts before God and were not disappointed. When they could see no way whatever out of their great difficulty, help often came in an unexpected way, and none so far as

we have learned, were disappointed. The Lord says:
"Call on me in the day of trouble and I will answer
thee."

Wonderful is the power of prayer. The Spirit
of the Lord has been poured out upon many who
have attended that Prayer Meeting. It has been a
help and comfort to thousands, and a blessing to
their homes. In that great City it has been like an oasis
in a arid desert. This is not reflecting upon the
church, which no doubt is, and has been, doing good
w k; but shows that God has signally blessed that
Prayer Meeting to the glory of His Holy name. A revival exists in any place where God is pouring out His
holy spirit upon the people. This Prayer Meeting began with a few praying people, but increased greatly,
and developed into one of the greatest revivals of
modern time.

I remember one great Revival in P. E. I. It
occurred in 1874, at Valleyfield, during the Commun-
ion Season, and in the month of July, when nature is
robed in her loveliest garment. At that time the
Lord's Supper was observed there but once a year.
The people kept open houses, and many came from
far and near to be present at the feast. The occasion
indeed bore some resemblance to the feast of Weeks:
"And thou shalt rejoice before the Lord thy God,
thou and thy Son, and thy daughter, and thy man-
servant, and thy maid-servant, and the stranger, and
the fatherless, and the wid   that is among you, etc."
—Deut. 16: 11.

The conversation of the people was spiritual, and
there were great searchings of heart. The services
continued five days, beginning on Thursday and end-
ing on Monday. Prayer Meetings were held morning
and evening after preaching services, and also in the
houses. There were many men living there then who
were mighty in prayer.

At that season it pleased the Lord to pour out His spirit upon many. Where earnest holy men and women are, there revivals will be. The incidents of that occasion are most vivid in the writer's mind. Men and women, young men and maidens, were convicted of sin, and cried to God for mercy ; and having been saved, began to praise and magnify the Lord. People might be seen praying in the fields, along fences, in the woods, in barns and houses, as well as in the church. Soon the whole place was alive with prayers and praises. The world was but little thought of by those enjoying such rich blessings. They would sit up late at night to converse on what Christ did for them, and how he saved their souls. It was altogether a most glorious time, and in answer to prayer. Soon the Revival spread far and wide. It was not confined to the locality in which it began. The Holy Spirit works where and how he wills. Times of refreshing come from the presence of the Lord.

Cornelius was a man of earnest prayer and devout life ; a proselyte to the Jewish religion. An Angel from God was sent to speak to him. He was told what he should do, and he did it. He sent for Peter, and in the mean time gathered into his house his "kinsmen and friends". There was great expectation among them and many prayers sent up. Cornelius was without doubt praying. He was a praying man ; and when Peter was addressing them on spiritual matters, namely, the death, sufferings, and resurrection of Christ, and salvation through Him, the Holy Spirit fell on them that heard the word, and they spoke with other tongues and magnified God. The Holy Spirit revives those who are spiritually dead. A blessed revival was the result of prayer and preaching.

When the Comforter takes possession of men's hearts, He is said to fall upon them—(Acts 8 : 16) ; and they are said to receive the Holy Ghost.—(Acts 8 : 17.)

If we are going to have glorious Revivals we must first get our own hearts filled with the Holy Spirit. We must in order to do that pray much, be much at the throne of grace. God's children must be intensely in earnest, if they are going to have the church revived. This blessing will come in answer to prayer and supplication. The church is languishing around us at the very present time, 1912. The great need of the Church is a glorious revival, an out-pouring of the Spirit upon her. The ground is parched enough. Oh! that the spiritual showers would come down and we be refreshed, and our fields become fruitful. As the sunshine and showers bring out the grass and flowers, and clothe the trees with fruit and foliage, so the spirit of the Lord will beautify the Church with the beauties of grace and holiness. "The desert shall rejoice and blossom as the rose."—Isa. 35 : 1.

The promise of our Heavenly Father is to give the Holy Spirit to them that ask Him. Behold I send the promise of my Father upon you.—John 24 : 49. What the Father promises Christ promises. But we must be prepared to receive the Spirit, there must be in us earnest desire for the Spirit ere He will be poured out upon us. If there is going to be a glorious out-pouring of the Spirit upon individuals and assemblies, it will be in answer to prayer and supplication. The seeking, the praying and the waiting for the Spirit is ours. How blessed to be filled with the spirit of holiness, peace and love.

> Come Holy Spirit, love divine,
> In these dark hearts of ours to shine;
> Kindle in us a flame of love,
> The same as in the throne above.

Mitchell Bros., Printers, Charlottetown.

CPSIA information can be obtained
at www.ICGtesting.com
Printed in the USA
LVHW060824030623
748815LV00032B/717